conte...

British & North American Readers:
Please note that Australian cup and
spoon measurements are metric. A quick
conversion guide appears on page 63.
A glossary explaining unfamiliar terms
and ingredients begins on page 60.

When choosing meat for casseroles, don't make the mistake of thinking that the best quality meat will make the best casserole. The most expensive cuts of meat are usually the leanest and absolutely lean meat makes a dry casserole.

What you need is a well-marbled piece of meat, such as chuck steak or round steak, or if using lamb, shanks or chump chops. Because of the long slow cooking, they will become beautifully tender and succulent, never dry and cardboardy. You'll need to cut off quite a bit of fat from chuck or round steak. Make allowances for this when purchasing.

When choosing chicken, go for drumsticks or thighs instead of the leaner breast. Chicken breast dries out if cooked for a long time while the richer, darker meat of the thigh becomes very tender. When cutting a thigh fillet for casseroles, cut lengthways with the grain, rather than across the fillet. This helps the chicken to keep its shape and produces a more tender dish.

The best way to thicken a casserole is to flour the pieces of meat, shake off excess flour and brown them on all sides. The flour will give the meat a crunchy coating that will seal in its juices. When liquid is added to the dish the flour will thicken it, and because it is cooked for a long time, it will turn into a delicious blended sauce.

To brown meat for a casserole, heat butter or oil (or a mixture of the two) in a heavy-based pan and add the floured pieces of meat, a few at a time. Turn them to brown them well on all sides. They should be golden brown in colour and well sealed. Remove from the pan and put aside on a plate while you cook the rest of the meat. If you try to cook too many pieces at once they will stew rather than brown.

To ensure your casserole is as lean as possible, cook it a day in advance, and once it has cooled, spoon it into a dish, cover with plastic wrap and refrigerate overnight. Next day, carefully lift off the layer of fat that will have formed on top and discard.

Gently reheat the casserole and serve. Not only will this make your casserole almost entirely fat-free but it will actually improve its taste because the flavours have been allowed to meld.

4 coriander chicken
and rice casserole

8 Chinese dried mushrooms

1 tablespoon coriander seeds

cooking oil spray

8 (1.3kg) lean chicken thigh cutlets, skin removed

2 cups (400g) white long-grain rice

2 medium (300g) onions, sliced

4 cloves garlic, crushed

1 teaspoon ground turmeric

2¾ cups (680ml) boiling chicken stock

2 tablespoons fish sauce

1 tablespoon chopped fresh coriander leaves

Place mushrooms in small heatproof bowl, cover with boiling water, stand 20 minutes; drain. Discard stems; slice caps finely. Crush coriander seeds, using blade of large knife.
Coat 2.5-litre (10-cup) flameproof casserole dish with cooking oil spray; cook chicken, in batches, until browned both sides. Add rice, onion, garlic, crushed coriander seeds and turmeric to same dish, stir until fragrant. Add mushrooms, stock and fish sauce.
Place chicken over rice mixture; bake, covered, in moderately hot oven about 45 minutes or until rice is tender. Stir in fresh coriander.

Per serve fat 14.1g; fibre 4.7g; kJ 2851

pork and **bean**

casserole with polenta

Coat 2-litre (8-cup) flameproof casserole dish with cooking oil spray; cook pork, in batches, until browned all over.
Cook onion and garlic in same dish, stirring, until onion is soft. Return pork to dish with juice, water and crumbled stock cube; bring to boil.
Bake, covered, in moderate oven about 1 hour or until pork is tender. Stir in 4-bean mix, polenta, parsley and chives; bake, covered, about 15 minutes or until mixture has thickened.

cooking oil spray

800g lean diced pork

1 medium (150g) onion, chopped

1 clove garlic, crushed

3 cups (750ml) vegetable juice

1/2 cup (125ml) water

1 chicken stock cube

440g can 4-bean mix, rinsed, drained

1/4 cup (40g) polenta

2 tablespoons chopped fresh parsley

1 tablespoon chopped fresh chives

Per serve fat 4.5g; fibre 5.9g; kJ 1463

beef and pasta
country casserole

750g lean beef chuck
steak

cooking oil spray

5 small (400g) onions,
quartered

2 cloves garlic,
crushed

2 medium (240g)
carrots, chopped

1 cup (250ml) dry
red wine

3 cups (750ml) beef
stock

1/2 cup (125ml) tomato
paste

3 medium (360g)
zucchini, sliced thickly

2 cups (180g) spiral
pasta

Cut beef into 3cm cubes. Coat 2.5-litre (10-cup) flameproof casserole
dish with cooking oil spray; cook beef, in batches, until browned all over.
Cook onion and garlic in same dish, stirring, until onion is soft. Return
beef to dish with carrot, wine, stock and paste; bring to boil.
Bake, covered, in moderate oven about 1 1/2 hours or until beef is tender.
Add zucchini, bake, covered, about 20 minutes or until zucchini is tender.
Meanwhile, cook pasta in large pan of boiling water, uncovered, until just
tender; drain. Add to beef; stir until heated through.

Per serve fat 10.5g; fibre 8.2g; kJ 2114

lamb with rosemary
and vegetables

2 cloves garlic, crushed

4 (1kg) lean lamb leg chops

cooking oil spray

1 medium (350g) leek, chopped

4 baby (100g) onions, halved

2 medium (250g) parsnips, chopped

1 medium (400g) kumara, chopped

1/2 cup (125ml) dry red wine

1/2 cup (125ml) beef stock

2 tablespoons tomato paste

2 medium (240g) zucchini, chopped

2 teaspoons chopped fresh rosemary

Rub garlic over lamb. Coat 3-litre (12-cup) flameproof casserole dish with cooking oil spray; cook lamb until browned both sides. Add leek, onion, parsnip, kumara, wine, stock and paste to dish; bring to boil.

Bake, covered, in moderate oven 1½ hours, stirring occasionally. Stir in zucchini and rosemary; bake, covered, about 30 minutes or until lamb and zucchini are tender.

Per serve fat 14.6g; fibre 6.7g; kJ 1822

hungarian-style
goulash

800g lean diced veal

1 tablespoon sweet paprika

2 tablespoons plain flour

2 teaspoons caraway seeds

cooking oil spray

1 medium (150g) onion, chopped

1 cup (250ml) beef stock

2 x 400g cans tomatoes

1 tablespoon tomato paste

3 medium (600g) potatoes, chopped

2 teaspoons chopped fresh oregano

Toss veal in combined paprika, flour and seeds; shake off excess. Coat 2.5-litre (10-cup) flameproof casserole dish with cooking oil spray; cook veal, in batches, until browned all over. Cook onion in same dish, stirring, until soft. Return veal to dish with stock, undrained crushed tomatoes and paste; bring to boil.

Bake, covered, in moderate oven 45 minutes. Add potato; bake, covered, 45 minutes or until potato and veal are tender. Stir in oregano.

Per serve fat 4.8g;
fibre 6.1g;
kJ1577

We used a clay pot, purchased from an Asian food store. Soak it in cold water overnight before using.

8 (880g) lean chicken thigh fillets, halved

2 small (160g) onions, quartered

500g baby bok choy, chopped roughly

½ cup (125ml) chicken stock

marinade

4 cloves garlic, crushed

1 tablespoon fish sauce

1 tablespoon soy sauce

1 tablespoon hoi sin sauce

2 tablespoons lime juice

2 tablespoons finely chopped fresh lemon grass

Combine chicken and Marinade in large bowl. Cover; refrigerate 3 hours or overnight.

Place undrained chicken and remaining ingredients in 2.5-litre (10-cup) clay pot or casserole dish; mix gently.

Bake, covered, in moderate oven about 1 hour or until chicken is tender.

Marinade Combine all ingredients in small bowl; mix well.

Per serve fat 10g; fibre 5.5g; kJ 1515

12 hot and spicy
chicken and kumara

8 (1.3kg) lean chicken thigh cutlets, skin removed

1/4 cup (35g) plain flour

2 teaspoons ground cumin

2 teaspoons sweet paprika

2 teaspoons ground turmeric

cooking oil spray

1 medium (150g) onion, quartered

1 medium (120g) carrot, sliced

2 cloves garlic, crushed

1 teaspoon sambal oelek

1½ cups (375ml) chicken stock

1/4 cup chopped fresh coriander leaves

1 medium (400g) kumara, chopped

2 tablespoons light sour cream

Toss chicken in combined flour and spices, reserve remaining flour mixture.
Coat 2.5-litre (10-cup) flameproof casserole dish with cooking oil spray; cook chicken, in batches, until browned both sides.
Cook onion, carrot, garlic and sambal oelek in same dish, stirring, until onion is soft. Add reserved flour mixture to dish; cook, stirring, until mixture thickens and bubbles. Gradually add stock, stirring constantly until mixture boils and thickens.
Return chicken to dish; bake, covered, in moderate oven 30 minutes. Add coriander and kumara; bake, uncovered, about 20 minutes or until kumara and chicken are tender. Add cream.

Per serve fat 15.8g; fibre 4.8g; kJ 1815

minted veal
with baby squash

cooking oil spray

8 (1.4kg) lean veal loin chops

2 medium (300g) onions, sliced

3 cloves garlic, crushed

2 teaspoons ground turmeric

4 cardamom pods, bruised

1 teaspoon ground nutmeg

1 teaspoon grated lemon rind

1 tablespoon tomato paste

2 tablespoons chopped fresh mint leaves

2 cups (500ml) beef stock

200g baby yellow squash, halved

1 tablespoon cornflour

2 tablespoons water

Per serve fat 4.8g; fibre 3.5g; kJ 1264

Coat 2.5-litre (10-cup) flameproof casserole dish with cooking oil spray; cook veal, in batches, until browned both sides. Cook onion, garlic and spices in same dish, stirring, until onion is soft. Return veal to dish with rind, paste, mint and stock; bring to boil.

Bake, covered, in moderate oven about 45 minutes or until veal is tender. Add squash; bake, uncovered, about 15 minutes or until squash are almost tender. Add blended cornflour and water; bake, uncovered, about 10 minutes or until mixture has thickened slightly, stirring occasionally.

octopus in
tomato sauce

1kg baby octopus

cooking oil spray

1 medium (150g) onion, chopped finely

2 cloves garlic, crushed

1/3 cup (80ml) dry white wine

2 x 400g cans tomatoes

2 tablespoons tomato paste

1 tablespoon finely chopped drained anchovies

1 teaspoon sugar

Remove and discard heads and beaks from octopus. Coat 2-litre (8-cup) flameproof casserole dish with cooking oil spray; cook onion and garlic, stirring, until onion is soft.

Add octopus; cook over high heat until octopus has changed colour. Add wine, undrained crushed tomatoes, paste, anchovies and sugar; bring to boil.

Bake, covered, in moderate oven 1 hour. Uncover; bake about 30 minutes or until octopus are tender.

Per serve fat 3.4g; fibre 3.6g; kJ 836

paprika
chicken

cooking oil spray

6 (1kg) lean chicken thigh cutlets, skin removed, halved

2 medium (300g) onions, sliced

4 cloves garlic, crushed

1 tablespoon sweet paprika

250g button mushrooms, sliced

400g can tomatoes

¼ cup (60ml) tomato paste

2 tablespoons light sour cream

Coat 2-litre (8-cup) flameproof casserole dish with cooking oil spray; cook chicken, in batches, until browned all over. Cook onion, garlic, paprika and mushrooms in same dish, stirring, until onion is soft. Return chicken to dish with undrained crushed tomatoes and paste; bring to boil. **Bake**, covered, in moderate oven about 1 hour or until chicken is tender. Just before serving, stir in cream.

Per serve fat 13g; fibre 5.7g; kJ 1329

almond, chickpea
and pumpkin casserole

cooking oil spray

900g butternut pumpkin, chopped

1 large (500g) leek, sliced

575g bottled tomato pasta sauce

1 cup (250ml) water

425g can chickpeas, drained

1 tablespoon lemon juice

1 tablespoon ground cumin

1/2 cup (70g) slivered almonds, toasted

200ml low-fat yogurt

2 tablespoons finely chopped fresh mint leaves

Coat 2-litre (8-cup) flameproof casserole dish with cooking oil spray; cook pumpkin and leek, stirring, until leek is soft. Add sauce, water, chickpeas, juice and cumin; bring to boil.

Bake, covered, in moderate oven about 30 minutes or until pumpkin is tender, stirring occasionally. Stir in nuts; serve with combined yogurt and mint.

Per serve fat 14.9g; fibre 12.9g; kJ 1628

18 beef ragout

800g lean beef chuck steak

plain flour

cooking oil spray

2 cloves garlic, crushed

4 slices (60g) pancetta, chopped

1 1/2 cups (375ml) dry red wine

1/2 cup (125ml) beef stock

1 1/2 tablespoons tomato paste

1 tablespoon Dijon mustard

1 tablespoon chopped fresh thyme

4 medium (480g) carrots, chopped roughly

1 bunch (400g) spring onions, halved

Cut beef into 3cm cubes. Toss beef in flour, shake off excess. Coat 2.5-litre (10-cup) flameproof casserole dish with cooking oil spray; cook beef, in batches, until browned all over. Cook garlic and pancetta in same dish, stirring, until pancetta is crisp. Return beef to dish with wine, stock, paste, mustard, thyme and carrot; bring to boil.
Bake, covered, in moderate oven about 2 hours or until beef is very tender. Add onions; bake, covered, about 30 minutes or until onions are soft.

Per serve fat 10.9g; fibre 5.9g; kJ 1770

veal and eggplant
casserole

1 large (500g) eggplant

cooking oil spray

2 medium (300g) onions, sliced

4 cloves garlic, crushed

600g lean diced veal

plain flour

300g button mushrooms, sliced

425g can tomato puree

1 tablespoon tomato paste

1 teaspoon sugar

¼ cup (60ml) dry white wine

2 tablespoons chopped fresh oregano

1 tablespoon chopped fresh basil leaves

Cut eggplant into 2cm pieces, sprinkle all over with salt; stand, in single layer, 20 minutes. Rinse eggplant thoroughly under cold water; drain. Pat dry with absorbent paper.

Coat 2.5-litre (10-cup) flameproof casserole dish with cooking oil spray; cook onion and garlic, stirring, until onion is soft. Toss veal in flour, shake off excess. Add veal to onion mixture in dish; cook, stirring, until veal is browned lightly.

Add eggplant, mushrooms, puree, paste, sugar and wine; bring to boil.

Bake, covered, in moderate oven 45 minutes. Stir in herbs; bake, covered about 15 minutes or until veal is tender.

Per serve fat 4g; fibre 9.1g; kJ 1319

curried

lamb casserole

800g lean diced lamb

plain flour

cooking oil spray

2 medium (300g) onions, chopped

2 medium (240g) carrots, sliced

2 sticks celery, sliced

1 teaspoon mild curry powder

1 teaspoon ground cumin

1 teaspoon ground coriander

1 teaspoon garam masala

1/4 cup (60ml) fruit chutney

1 cup (250ml) water

1 beef stock cube

1/4 cup (60ml) dry red wine

1 1/2 tablespoons cornflour

1/4 cup (60ml) water, extra

Toss lamb in flour, shake off excess. Coat 2-litre (8-cup) flameproof casserole dish with cooking oil spray; cook lamb, in batches, until browned all over. Cook onion, carrot, celery and spices in same dish, stirring, until fragrant. Return lamb to dish with chutney, water, crumbled stock cube and wine; bring to boil.

Bake, covered, in moderate oven about 2 hours or until lamb is tender. Stir in blended cornflour and extra water; bake, covered, about 10 minutes or until thickened slightly.

Per serve fat 8.7g; fibre 5.3g; kJ 1646

boeuf bourguignon

800g lean beef chuck steak

cooking oil spray

400g baby onions

2 cloves garlic, crushed

1 bacon rasher, fat removed, chopped

200g button mushrooms

1¹/₂ tablespoons tomato paste

1 cup (250ml) dry red wine

¹/₃ cup (80ml) port

¹/₄ cup (60 ml) beef stock

Cut beef into 3cm cubes. Coat 2-litre (8-cup) flameproof casserole dish with cooking oil spray; cook beef, in batches, until browned all over. Cook onions, garlic and bacon in same dish, stirring, until onions are soft. Return beef and any juices to dish with remaining ingredients; bring to boil.

Bake, covered, in moderate oven 2 hours. Uncover; bake about 30 minutes or until beef is very tender and sauce has thickened slightly.

Per serve fat 11.2g; fibre 3.3g; kJ 1600

24 veal with spinach
and mushrooms

cooking oil spray

800g lean diced veal

1 medium (350g) leek, sliced

1 teaspoon chopped fresh thyme

1/4 cup (60ml) dry white wine

1 chicken stock cube

400g can tomatoes

250g button mushrooms

1 small (150g) red capsicum, chopped

250g spinach, trimmed, chopped roughly

2 tablespoons shredded fresh basil leaves

Coat 2.5-litre (10-cup) flameproof casserole dish with cooking oil spray; cook veal, in batches, until browned all over. Return veal to dish with leek and thyme; cook, stirring, until leek is soft. Stir in wine, crumbled stock cube, undrained crushed tomatoes, mushrooms and capsicum; bring to boil.

Bake, covered, in moderate oven about 2 hours or until veal is very tender. Just before serving, stir in spinach and basil.

Per serve fat 4.5g; fibre 5.6g; kJ 1193

cajun-style
seafood gumbo

250g okra

800g boneless white fish fillets

40 (1kg) medium uncooked prawns

cooking oil spray

1 bacon rasher, fat removed, chopped

1 medium (150g) onion, chopped finely

2 cloves garlic, crushed

1 tablespoon plain flour

1½ cups (375ml) fish stock

400g can tomatoes

1 tablespoon tomato paste

1 teaspoon Tabasco sauce

2 teaspoons Worcestershire sauce

310g can corn kernels, drained

Trim stems from okra; cut fish into 3cm pieces; shell and devein prawns, leaving tails intact.
Coat 3-litre (12-cup) flameproof casserole dish with cooking oil spray; cook bacon, stirring, until crisp, drain on absorbent paper. Cook onion and garlic in same dish, stirring, until onion is soft. Add flour; cook, stirring, until mixture is browned lightly. Gradually stir in stock, undrained crushed tomatoes, paste, sauces, corn and okra; stir until mixture boils and thickens slightly.
Bake, uncovered, in moderate oven about 40 minutes or until okra is tender, stirring occasionally. Stir in seafood and bacon; bake, uncovered, about 15 minutes or until tender.

Per serve fat 9.4g; fibre 6.4g; kJ 1962

beef, potato and
rosemary ragout

Cut beef and kumara into 3cm cubes. Coat 2.5-litre (10-cup) flameproof casserole dish with cooking oil spray; cook beef, in batches, until browned all over. Return beef to dish with bacon, onion and garlic; cook, stirring, until onion is soft. Stir in puree, stock, wine, rosemary and sauce; bring to boil.

Bake, covered, in moderate oven about 1¹/₂ hours or until beef is just tender. Stir in kumara, potato and blended flour and water; bake, uncovered, about 30 minutes or until vegetables and beef are tender. Discard rosemary sprig.

800g lean beef chuck steak

1 medium (400g) kumara

cooking oil spray

1 bacon rasher, fat removed, chopped

2 medium (300g) onions, chopped

2 cloves garlic, crushed

¹/₂ cup (125ml) tomato puree

1 cup (250ml) beef stock

¹/₃ cup (80ml) dry red wine

10cm sprig fresh rosemary

1 tablespoon Worcestershire sauce

12 tiny (480g) new potatoes, quartered

2 tablespoons plain flour

³/₄ cup (180ml) water

Per serve fat 11.5g; fibre 5.8g; kJ 1958

country-style

beef and mushrooms

1 large (350g) red capsicum

cooking oil spray

800g lean beef blade steak, chopped

1 clove garlic, crushed

1 small (300g) fennel bulb, sliced

100g button mushrooms, quartered

100g Swiss brown mushrooms, halved

100g shiitake mushrooms, sliced

1½ cups (375ml) beef stock

¼ cup (50g) barley

250g spinach, trimmed, shredded

Quarter capsicum, remove seeds and membrane. Roast under grill or in very hot oven, skin side up, until skin blisters and blackens. Cover capsicum pieces in plastic or paper for 5 minutes, peel away skin, cut flesh into thin strips.

Coat 2.5-litre (10-cup) flameproof casserole dish with cooking oil spray; cook beef, in batches, until browned all over. Cook garlic, fennel and mushrooms in same dish, stirring, until fennel is tender. Return beef to dish with capsicum, stock and barley; bring to boil.

Bake, covered, in moderate oven about 1½ hours or until beef is tender. Add spinach, stir until wilted.

Per serve fat 14.6g; fibre 6.4g; kJ 1603

chicken tagine

with dates and honey

8 (880g) lean chicken thigh fillets

cooking oil spray

2 medium (300g) onions, sliced thinly

4 cloves garlic, crushed

1 teaspoon cumin seeds

1½ teaspoons ground coriander

1 teaspoon ground turmeric

1 teaspoon ground cinnamon

½ teaspoon chilli powder

1½ cups (375ml) chicken stock

1 cup (250ml) water

½ cup (85g) seedless dates, halved

¼ cup (60ml) honey

¼ cup (40g) blanched almonds, toasted

1 tablespoon chopped fresh coriander leaves

Cut chicken into 3cm strips. Coat 2.5-litre (10-cup) flameproof casserole dish with cooking oil spray; cook chicken, in batches, until browned all over. Cook onion, garlic and spices in same dish, stirring, until onion is soft. Return chicken to dish with stock and water; bring to boil. Bake, covered, in moderate oven 1 hour. Uncover; bake about 45 minutes or until chicken is very tender and mixture has thickened slightly. Stir in dates, honey and nuts; sprinkle with fresh coriander.

Per serve fat 16.2g; fibre 5.1g; kJ 2025

braised chicken with
lentils and sage

8 (1.2kg) lean chicken drumsticks, skin removed

plain flour

cooking oil spray

2 large (360g) carrots, chopped roughly

1 medium (150g) onion, chopped roughly

1 1/2 cups (375ml) chicken stock

1/2 cup (125ml) tomato puree

4 medium (480g) zucchini, sliced thickly

1/2 cup (100g) red lentils

1 tablespoon chopped fresh sage leaves

Toss chicken in flour, shake off excess. Coat 2.5-litre (10-cup) flameproof casserole dish with cooking oil spray; cook chicken, in batches, until browned all over. Cook carrot and onion in same dish, stirring, until onion is soft. Return chicken to dish with stock and tomato puree; bring to boil.

Bake, covered, in moderate oven 20 minutes. Stir in zucchini, lentils and sage; bake, covered, about 30 minutes or until lentils and chicken are tender, stirring occasionally.

Per serve fat 11.9g; fibre 9.9g; kJ 1689

tagine of beef

with tomatoes

800g lean beef chuck steak

1 medium (300g) eggplant

cooking oil spray

1 medium (150g) onion, sliced thinly

2 cloves garlic, crushed

$1/2$ teaspoon ground turmeric

$1/2$ teaspoon ground coriander

$1/4$ teaspoon ground cinnamon

$1/4$ teaspoon ground ginger

1 teaspoon cumin seeds

$1 1/4$ cups (310ml) beef stock

2 large (500g) tomatoes, peeled, chopped

$1/4$ cup (40g) seeded dates, halved

2 tablespoons blanched almonds, toasted

1 tablespoon honey

$1/4$ cup chopped fresh flat-leaf parsley

Cut beef into 3cm cubes. Cut eggplant into 1cm slices, sprinkle with salt; stand, in single layer, 20 minutes. Rinse, drain, pat dry with absorbent paper and cut each slice into quarters.

Coat 2.5-litre (10-cup) flameproof casserole dish with cooking oil spray; cook beef, in batches, until browned all over. Cook onion, garlic and spices in same dish, stirring, until onion is soft. Return beef to dish with stock and tomato; bring to boil.

Bake, covered, in moderate oven $1 1/4$ hours. Add eggplant; bake uncovered, 45 minutes. Stir in remaining ingredients.

Per serve fat 12.3g; fibre 5.5g; kJ 1515

purees and
mashes

Roasted pumpkin mash

Parsnip and potato puree

Green pea mash

parsnip and potato puree

2 medium (250g) parsnips, peeled, chopped

2 medium (400g) potatoes, peeled, chopped

2 tablespoons skim milk

10g butter

2 teaspoons chopped fresh thyme

Boil, steam or microwave parsnips and potatoes separately until tender. **Process** parsnips until smooth. Mash potatoes with milk and butter until almost smooth. Add to parsnip puree in processor, process until just combined. Stir in thyme.

Per serve fat 2.2g; fibre 2.7g; kJ 438

roasted pumpkin mash

2kg butternut pumpkin, peeled, chopped

cooking oil spray

2 tablespoons buttermilk

1/4 cup (20g) finely grated parmesan cheese

1/4 teaspoon ground nutmeg

Coat pumpkin with cooking oil spray, add to non-stick baking dish; bake, uncovered, in hot oven about 1 hour or until pumpkin is tender and browned lightly.
Transfer pumpkin to large bowl. Working quickly, mash pumpkin then push through fine sieve back into same bowl. Stir in remaining ingredients and serve immediately.

Per serve fat 4.2g; fibre 4.9g; kJ 788

green pea mash

You will need approximately 2.5kg unshelled green peas (about 1kg shelled) for this recipe

6 cups shelled green peas

1/4 cup (20g) finely grated parmesan cheese

1/3 cup (80ml) light cream

1 teaspoon cracked black pepper

Boil, steam or microwave peas until just tender; drain. **Blend** or process peas with remaining ingredients.
Per serve fat 7.1g; fibre 14g; kJ 915

garlic potato mash

5 medium (1kg) potatoes, peeled, chopped

2 chicken stock cubes

10g butter

1/2 cup (125ml) buttermilk

1 clove garlic, crushed

Add potatoes to large pan of boiling water; boil, uncovered, until tender, drain. Mash potatoes with crumbled stock cubes and remaining ingredients. Serve hot.
Per serve fat 3g; fibre 3.5g; kJ 748

Below: Garlic potato mash

pork with **prunes**

and cabbage

800g lean pork neck

plain flour

cooking oil spray

1 medium (150g) onion, chopped

2 cloves garlic, crushed

1/4 cup (60ml) brandy

3 1/2 cups (875ml) chicken stock

1/2 cup (105g) chopped seeded prunes

2 tablespoons chopped fresh oregano

1 tablespoon chopped fresh thyme

2 1/2 cups (200g) shredded cabbage

Cut pork into 3cm cubes. Toss pork in flour, shake off excess. Coat 3-litre (12-cup) flameproof casserole dish with cooking oil spray; cook pork, in batches, until browned all over. Cook onion and garlic in same dish, stirring, until onion is soft. Return pork to dish with brandy, stock, prunes and herbs; bring to boil. Stir in cabbage.

Bake, covered, in moderate oven about 1 hour or until pork is tender.

Per serve fat 4.6g; fibre 5.2g; kJ 1546

chilli

con carne

800g lean beef chuck
steak

cooking oil spray

2 medium (300g)
onions, sliced

2 medium (400g) red
capsicums, chopped

3 cloves garlic,
crushed

1 small fresh red chilli,
chopped finely

2 teaspoons ground
cumin

2 teaspoons ground
coriander

1 teaspoon chilli
powder

2 x 400g cans
tomatoes

1/4 cup (60ml) tomato
paste

1 cup (250ml) beef
stock

300g can red kidney
beans, rinsed, drained

Cut beef into 3cm cubes. Coat 2.5-litre (10-cup)
flameproof casserole dish with cooking oil
spray; cook beef, in batches, until browned all
over. Cook onion, capsicum, garlic and chilli in
same dish, stirring, until onion is browned
lightly. Add spices; cook, stirring, until fragrant.
Return beef and any juices to dish with
undrained crushed tomatoes, paste and stock;
bring to boil.
Bake, covered, in moderate oven 1 1/2 hours.
Add kidney beans; bake, uncovered, about 30
minutes or until beef is tender and sauce has
thickened slightly.

Per serve fat 11.2g;
fibre 9.3g; kJ 1622

aussie

beef curry

800g lean beef round steak

cooking oil spray

1 large (200g) onion, chopped

1 tablespoon grated fresh ginger

1 tablespoon mild curry powder

1/2 teaspoon ground turmeric

1/2 teaspoon ground coriander

3 cups (750ml) beef stock

2 medium (300g) apples, peeled, chopped

2 tablespoons fruit chutney

1 tablespoon desiccated coconut

1/2 cup (80g) sultanas

1/4 cup chopped fresh coriander leaves

banana sambal

2 small (260g) bananas, sliced

1 teaspoon lemon juice

1/4 cup (20g) desiccated coconut

Cut beef into 3cm cubes. Coat 2-litre (8-cup) flameproof casserole dish with cooking oil spray; cook beef, in batches, until browned all over. Cook onion, ginger, curry powder and spices in same dish, stirring, until onion is soft. Return beef to dish with stock, apple, fruit chutney, coconut and sultanas; bring to boil.

Bake, covered, in moderate oven 1 1/2 hours. Uncover; bake about 30 minutes or until beef is tender and sauce has thickened slightly. Stir in fresh coriander; serve with Banana Sambal.

Banana Sambal Combine banana and juice in small bowl; toss with coconut.

Per serve fat 13.5g; fibre 6.2g; kJ 1956

beef
olives

250g lean minced pork and veal

1 tablespoon chopped fresh parsley

2 cloves garlic, crushed

750g thinly sliced lean beef rump steaks

cooking oil spray

400g can tomatoes

1 beef stock cube

$1/2$ cup (125ml) dry red wine

1 teaspoon sugar

1 teaspoon seasoned pepper

2 tablespoons cornflour

$1/4$ cup (60ml) water

Combine pork and veal mince, parsley and garlic in medium bowl; mix well. Flatten beef steaks to 5mm thickness, using a mallet; cut into eight 7 x 15cm strips. Spoon pork and veal mixture onto centre of beef strips, roll up from short sides to enclose filling; secure with toothpicks.

Coat 2-litre (8-cup) flameproof casserole dish with cooking oil spray; cook beef olives, in batches, until browned all over. Return beef olives to dish with undrained crushed tomatoes, crumbled stock cube, wine, sugar and pepper; bring to boil.

Bake, covered, in moderate oven 1 hour. Stir in blended cornflour and water; bake, covered, about 45 minutes or until beef is tender and sauce has thickened.

Per serve fat 9.6g; fibre 1.4g; kJ 1656

lamb and vegetable

casserole

cooking oil spray

800g lean diced lamb

1 medium (150g) onion, chopped

2 cloves garlic, crushed

3 medium (360g) carrots, chopped

2 sticks celery, sliced

2 tablespoons instant gravy mix

3 cups (750ml) water

3 large (600g) potatoes, chopped

2 tablespoons finely chopped fresh thyme

3/4 cup (90g) frozen peas, thawed

Coat 2.5-litre (10-cup) flameproof casserole dish with cooking oil spray; cook lamb, in batches, until browned all over. Cook onion and garlic in same dish, stirring, until onion is soft. Return lamb to dish with carrot and celery, stir in combined gravy mix and water; bring to boil.

Bake, covered, in moderate oven 1½ hours. Add potato and thyme; bake, covered, about 30 minutes or until potato is just tender. Stir in peas during last 5 minutes of cooking time.

Per serve fat 8.5g; fibre 7.8g; kJ 1690

indian-style
spiced chicken

cooking oil spray

8 (1.3kg) lean chicken thigh cutlets, skin removed

2 medium (300g) onions, chopped

2 small fresh red chillies, chopped

1 teaspoon ground cinnamon

2 teaspoons cumin seeds

1 tablespoon grated fresh ginger

2 cloves garlic, crushed

2 large (600g) potatoes, peeled, chopped

½ cup (125ml) water

3 small (390g) tomatoes, peeled, seeded, chopped

Coat 2.5-litre (10-cup) flameproof casserole dish with cooking oil spray; cook chicken, in batches, until browned both sides. Cook onion, chilli, cinnamon, seeds, ginger and garlic in same dish, stirring, until onion is soft. Return chicken to dish with potato, water and tomato; bring to boil.

Bake, covered, in moderate oven 30 minutes or until chicken and potato are tender.

Per serve fat 13.6g; fibre 4.8g; kJ 1729

spicy

vegetable casserole

cooking oil spray

2 medium (700g) leeks, chopped

2 cloves garlic, crushed

2 teaspoons mild curry powder

1/2 teaspoon ground cumin

1/2 teaspoon ground turmeric

1/2 small (500g) cauliflower, chopped

125g green beans, chopped

1 cup (125g) frozen peas, thawed

1/3 cup (65g) red lentils

1 vegetable stock cube

2 cups (500ml) boiling water

1/3 cup (55g) raisins

1 tablespoon chopped fresh coriander leaves

1 tablespoon cornflour

1 tablespoon water, extra

Per serve fat 2.5g; fibre 11.6g; kJ 788

Coat 2-litre (8-cup) flameproof casserole dish with cooking oil spray; cook leek, garlic, curry powder, cumin and turmeric, stirring, until leek is soft. Add cauliflower, beans, peas, lentils, crumbled stock cube, boiling water, raisins and fresh coriander.

Bake, covered, in moderate oven about 45 minutes or until vegetables are just tender. Stir in blended cornflour and extra water; bake, covered, about 10 minutes or until mixture has thickened slightly.

baked **eggplants**,

2 medium (600g)
eggplants, sliced

cooking oil spray

10 (250g) spring
onions, trimmed

2 cloves garlic,
crushed

3 sticks celery, sliced

2 x 300g cans
chickpeas, rinsed,
drained

4 large (1kg)
tomatoes, peeled,
chopped

1 tablespoon tomato
paste

1/2 cup (125ml)
vegetable stock

1/4 cup chopped fresh
parsley

1/4 cup chopped fresh
oregano

500g baby bok choy,
chopped

tomato and chickpeas

Grill eggplant slices until browned both sides. Coat 3-litre (12-cup) flameproof casserole dish with cooking oil spray; cook onions, stirring, until browned lightly. Add eggplant, garlic, celery, chickpeas, tomato, tomato paste, stock and herbs; bring to boil.

Bake, covered, in moderate oven about 45 minutes or until vegetables are tender. Add bok choy, stir until wilted.

Per serve fat 3.8g; fibre 15.2g; kJ 816

44 light and
spicy fish

Coat 2-litre (8-cup) flameproof casserole dish with cooking oil spray; cook onion and garlic, stirring, until onion is soft. Add spices; cook, stirring, until fragrant. Add undrained crushed tomatoes, potato and sugar; bring to boil. Bake, covered, in moderate oven about 20 minutes or until potato is tender. Add fish; bake, covered, about 15 minutes or until fish is cooked through. Serve sprinkled with parsley and nuts.

cooking oil spray

1 medium (150g) onion, chopped

2 cloves garlic, crushed

2 teaspoons sweet paprika

pinch cayenne pepper

2 teaspoons ground cumin

1 teaspoon ground coriander

2 x 400g cans tomatoes

1 large (300g) potato, chopped

1 teaspoon sugar

400g boneless white fish fillets, chopped roughly

2 tablespoons chopped fresh parsley

2 tablespoons toasted flaked almonds

Per serve fat 5.4g; fibre 5.2g; kJ 955

beef and **bean**

casserole

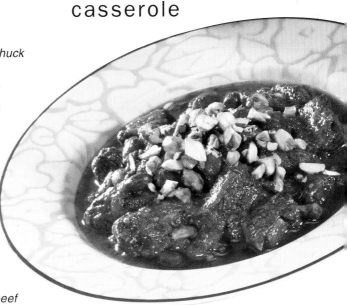

800g lean beef chuck steak

cooking oil spray

2 medium (300g) onions, sliced

3 cloves garlic, crushed

1 teaspoon ground ginger

$^{1}/_{2}$ teaspoon ground cinnamon

$^{1}/_{2}$ cup (125ml) dry sherry

2 cups (500ml) beef stock

$^{1}/_{2}$ cup (125ml) tomato paste

2 teaspoons sambal oelek

2 small dried red chillies, chopped

4 small (520g) tomatoes, peeled, halved

300g can red kidney beans, rinsed, drained

2 tablespoons toasted chopped pistachios

Cut beef into 4cm cubes. Coat 2.5-litre (10-cup) flameproof casserole dish with cooking oil spray; cook beef, in batches, until browned all over. Return beef to dish with onion and garlic; cook, stirring, until onion is soft. Add spices; cook, stirring, until fragrant. Add sherry, stock, paste and sambal oelek; bring to boil. Stir in chillies and tomato.

Bake, covered, in moderately hot oven 1 hour. Uncover; bake 30 minutes, stirring occasionally. Stir in beans; bake, uncovered, about 15 minutes or until beef is tender. Serve sprinkled with nuts.

Per serve fat 13.6g; fibre 8.3g; kJ 1762

46 lamb shanks with
barley in red wine

cooking oil spray

8 (1.5kg) lean French-trimmed lamb shanks

2 medium (300g) onions

3 cloves garlic, crushed

4 medium (480g) carrots, chopped

1/2 cup (65g) pearl barley, rinsed, drained

1 cup (250ml) dry red wine

1 cup (250ml) beef stock

400g can tomatoes

1/4 cup (60ml) tomato paste

1 tablespoon finely chopped fresh thyme

Coat medium flameproof baking dish with cooking oil spray; cook lamb, in batches, until browned all over. Halve onions lengthways; cut into thick wedges. Cook onion and garlic in same dish, stirring, until onion is soft.

Return lamb to dish with carrot, barley, wine, stock, undrained crushed tomatoes and paste; bring to boil.

Bake, covered, in moderate oven 2 hours, stirring occasionally. Stir in thyme; bake, uncovered, about 15 minutes or until lamb is very tender.

Per serve fat 6.4g; fibre 8.7g; kJ 1903

italian veal

casserole

cooking oil spray

800g lean diced veal

1 medium (150g) onion, chopped

2 cloves garlic, crushed

400g can tomatoes

1 chicken stock cube

1/2 cup (125ml) dry red wine

1/2 cup (125ml) water

1/2 cup (60g) seeded black olives, sliced

1 medium (200g) green capsicum, chopped

1 medium (200g) red capsicum, chopped

1/4 cup chopped fresh parsley

2 tablespoons chopped fresh basil leaves

1 tablespoon chopped fresh oregano

1 teaspoon chopped fresh thyme

Per serve fat 7.4g; fibre 3.7g; kJ 1271

Coat 2-litre (8-cup) flameproof casserole dish with cooking oil spray; cook veal, in batches, until browned all over. Cook onion and garlic in same dish, stirring, until onion is soft. Return veal to dish with undrained crushed tomatoes and remaining ingredients; bring to boil.
Bake, covered, in moderately slow oven about 1 3/4 hours or until veal is very tender.

and tomato curry

cooking oil spray

750g lean diced lamb

1 large (200g) onion, sliced

2 cloves garlic, crushed

1 small fresh red chilli, chopped finely

1/2 teaspoon garam masala

1/2 teaspoon ground coriander

1/2 teaspoon ground turmeric

1/4 cup chopped fresh mint leaves

1 1/2 tablespoons tomato paste

2 medium (380g) tomatoes, chopped

1 cup (250ml) beef stock

Coat 2-litre (8-cup) flameproof casserole dish with cooking oil spray; cook lamb, in batches, until browned all over. Cook onion and garlic in same dish, stirring, until onion is soft. Add chilli and spices; cook, stirring, until fragrant. Return lamb to dish with mint, paste, tomato and stock; bring to boil.

Bake, covered, in moderate oven about 1 1/2 hours or until lamb is tender.

Per serve fat 7.9g; fibre 2.7g; kJ 1128

french-onion
lamb chop casserole

cooking oil spray

8 (1kg) lean lamb chump chops

6 baby (150g) onions, halved

2 cloves garlic, crushed

2 small (400g) leeks, chopped

40g packet French onion soup mix

1½ cups (375ml) boiling water

1 tablespoon finely chopped fresh parsley

Coat medium flameproof baking dish with cooking oil spray; cook lamb, in batches, until browned both sides. Cook onion, garlic and leek in same dish, stirring, until onion is browned lightly. Return lamb to dish; sprinkle with soup mix, pour over water.

Bake, covered, in moderate oven 40 minutes. Uncover; bake about 30 minutes or until lamb is tender and sauce has thickened. Just before serving, sprinkle with parsley.

Per serve fat 14.3g; fibre 3.3g; kJ 1461

lentil and **beef**

casserole

Coat 2-litre (8-cup) flameproof casserole dish with cooking oil spray; cook beef and onion, stirring, until beef is browned. Add carrot, celery, undrained crushed tomatoes, crumbled stock cubes and water; bring to boil. **Bake**, covered, in moderate oven about 40 minutes or until vegetables are tender. Stir in lentils, wine, extra water, paste and sugar; bake, covered, about 20 minutes or until lentils are tender and mixture is thick. Stir in basil.

cooking oil spray

500g lean minced beef

2 medium (300g) onions, chopped

2 medium (240g) carrots, chopped

2 sticks celery, chopped

400g can tomatoes

2 beef stock cubes

1 cup (250ml) water

1 cup (200g) red lentils, rinsed, drained

1/4 cup (60ml) dry red wine

1 1/2 cups (375ml) water, extra

2 tablespoons tomato paste

2 teaspoons sugar

1/4 cup shredded fresh basil leaves

Per serve fat 9.7g; fibre 12.3g; kJ 1650

osso
bucco

8 (1kg) lean osso
bucco (veal shin)

plain flour

cooking oil spray

2 medium (300g)
onions, sliced

4 cloves garlic,
crushed

2 x 400g cans
tomatoes

½ cup (125ml) dry
white wine

1 cup (250ml) beef
stock

1 bay leaf

1 tablespoon chopped
fresh thyme

1 tablespoon chopped
fresh oregano

2 tablespoons
chopped fresh parsley

Toss veal in flour, shake off excess. Coat
2.5-litre (10-cup) flameproof casserole dish with
cooking oil spray; cook veal, in batches, until
browned all over. Cook onion and garlic in same
dish, stirring, until onion is soft. Return veal to
dish with undrained crushed tomatoes, wine,
stock, bay leaf, thyme and oregano; mix well
and bring to boil.

Bake, covered, in moderate oven 2 hours.
Uncover; bake about 1 hour or until veal is very
tender. Discard bay leaf; serve sprinkled with
chopped parsley.

Per serve fat 3.8g;
fibre 4.6g; kJ 1227

kumara-topped
lamb

750g lean diced lamb

plain flour

cooking oil spray

1 medium (350g) leek, sliced

1 medium (300g) eggplant, chopped

1 clove garlic, crushed

1/3 cup (80ml) beef stock

1/4 cup (60ml) tomato puree

1 teaspoon chopped fresh thyme

Sweet Potato
kumara topping

2 large (1kg) kumara, chopped

2 tablespoons light sour cream

2 tablespoons grated parmesan cheese

1 tablespoon chopped fresh parsley

Toss lamb in flour, shake off excess. Coat 1.5-litre (6-cup) flameproof casserole dish with cooking oil spray; cook lamb, in batches, until browned all over. Cook leek, eggplant and garlic in same dish, stirring, 5 minutes. Return lamb to dish with stock, puree and thyme; bring to boil. **Bake,** covered, in moderate oven about 1 hour or until lamb is just tender.

Spoon Kumara Topping into piping bag fitted with large star tube, pipe topping over lamb mixture. Bake, uncovered, in moderately hot oven about 30 minutes or until browned lightly.

Kumara Topping Boil, steam or microwave kumara until tender; drain. Process kumara with remaining ingredients until mixture is smooth.

Per serve fat 11.1g; fibre 8.2g; kJ 2049

veal
marengo

cooking oil spray

800g lean diced veal

1 medium (150g) onion, sliced

1 small (200g) leek, sliced

2 cloves garlic, crushed

1¹/₂ tablespoons tomato paste

1 teaspoon grated orange rind

¹/₂ cup (125ml) dry white wine

¹/₂ cup (125ml) beef stock

200g button mushrooms

¹/₃ cup (80ml) orange juice

2 medium (380g) tomatoes, peeled, seeded, chopped

Coat 2-litre (8-cup) flameproof casserole dish with cooking oil spray; cook veal, in batches, until browned all over. Cook onion, leek and garlic in same dish, stirring, until onion is soft. Return veal and any juices to dish with remaining ingredients; bring to boil.

Bake, covered, in moderate oven 1¹/₂ hours. Uncover; bake about 45 minutes or until veal is tender and sauce has thickened slightly.

Per serve fat 4.2g; fibre 4.4g; kJ 1222

veal

ratatouille casserole

8 (1.4kg) lean veal
cutlets

plain flour

cooking oil spray

1 medium (350g) leek,
chopped

2 cloves garlic,
crushed

1 medium (200g) red
capsicum, chopped

1 medium (200g)
green capsicum,
chopped

4 baby (240g)
eggplants, chopped

1/4 cup (60ml) dry
white wine

200g button
mushrooms

3 medium (360g)
zucchini, chopped

2 x 400g cans
tomatoes

425g can tomato
puree

2 tablespoons
chopped fresh
oregano

1/2 cup (80g) black
olives

2 teaspoons sugar

Toss veal in flour,
shake off excess.
Coat 4-litre (16-cup)
flameproof casserole
dish with cooking oil
spray; cook veal, in
batches, until
browned both sides.
Cook leek and garlic
in same dish, stirring,
until leek is soft.
Add capsicum and
eggplant; cook,
stirring, until eggplant
is soft. Add wine,
mushrooms and
zucchini; bring to boil,
simmer, uncovered,
until liquid has
reduced by half. Add
undrained crushed
tomatoes, puree and
oregano; bring to boil.
Bake, uncovered, in
moderate oven 20
minutes. Add veal;
bake, covered, about
45 minutes or until
veal is tender. Stir in
olives and sugar.

Per serve fat 9.9g;
fibre 12.4g; kJ 2165

lamb shanks with
spinach and basil

8 (2kg) lean lamb shanks

plain flour

cooking oil spray

2 medium (300g) onions, sliced

2 cloves garlic, crushed

3 large (540g) carrots, chopped

3 cups (750ml) chicken stock

1 tablespoon Dijon mustard

500g spinach, trimmed

¼ cup finely shredded fresh basil leaves

Toss lamb in flour, shake off excess. Coat medium flameproof baking dish with cooking oil spray; cook lamb, in batches, until browned all over. Cook onion and garlic in same dish, stirring, until onion is soft. Return lamb to dish with carrot, stock and mustard; bring to boil. **Bake**, covered, in moderate oven about 2 hours or until lamb is very tender, stirring occasionally. Add spinach and basil; stir until spinach is wilted.

Per serve fat 6.4g; fibre 7.4g; kJ 1683

lima bean casserole with

scalloped potato top

cooking oil spray

2 large (400g) onions,
sliced

2 cloves garlic,
crushed

2 teaspoons plain flour

2 cups (500ml)
vegetable stock

400g can tomatoes

1/2 cup (125ml) tomato
puree

1/4 cup (60ml) tomato
paste

1 teaspoon sugar

2 medium (240g)
carrots, chopped

1 stick celery, chopped

2 x 300g cans lima
beans, rinsed, drained

5 tiny (200g) new
potatoes

15g butter, melted

1/2 teaspoon cumin
seeds

Per serve fat 4.8g;
fibre 9.4g; kJ 749

Coat 1.5-litre (6-cup) flameproof casserole dish
with cooking oil spray; cook onion and garlic,
stirring, until onion is soft. Add flour; cook,
stirring, until mixture thickens and bubbles.
Gradually stir in stock, undrained crushed
tomatoes, puree, paste, sugar, carrot and
chopped celery.

Bake, covered, in moderate oven about
30 minutes or until carrot is tender. Stir in
beans. Cut potatoes into 2mm slices. Top bean
mixture with potato slices, brush with butter;
sprinkle with seeds. Bake, uncovered, in
moderately hot oven about 40 minutes or until
potato slices are browned lightly and tender.

58 veal cutlets, butterbeans and **COUSCOUS**

8 (1.4kg) lean veal cutlets

¼ cup (35g) plain flour

2 teaspoons sweet paprika

cooking oil spray

1 medium (170g) red onion, sliced

2 cloves garlic, crushed

¾ cup (180ml) beef stock

400g can tomatoes

¼ cup (15g) dry-packed sun-dried tomatoes

1 tablespoon chopped fresh oregano

300g can butter beans, rinsed, drained

couscous

1½ cups (300g) couscous

1¼ cups (310ml) boiling water

20g butter

1 tablespoon chopped fresh parsley

Per serve fat 12.9g; fibre 6.1g; kJ 2860

Toss veal in combined flour and paprika, shake off excess. Coat 2.5-litre (10-cup) flameproof casserole dish with cooking oil spray; cook veal, in batches, until browned both sides. Cook onion and garlic in same dish, stirring, until onion is soft. Return veal to dish with stock, undrained crushed canned tomatoes, sun-dried tomatoes and oregano; bring to boil.

Bake, covered, in moderate oven 45 minutes. Stir in beans; bake, covered, 15 minutes. Serve with Couscous.

Couscous Combine couscous, water and butter in large heatproof bowl; cover, stand about 5 minutes or until water is absorbed. Using fork, toss chopped parsley into couscous.

meatballs and
risoni in tomato sauce

750g lean minced beef

1 clove garlic, crushed

1/3 cup chopped fresh parsley

2 green onions, chopped

1 cup (70g) stale breadcrumbs

1 egg, lightly beaten

cooking oil spray

400g can tomatoes

300g can Tomato Supreme

1 1/2 cups (375ml) beef stock

1/2 cup (110g) risoni pasta

Per serve fat 14.7g;
fibre 4.7g; kJ 2012

Combine beef, garlic, parsley, onion, breadcrumbs and egg in large bowl; mix well. Shape quarter cups of mixture into balls.

Coat large non-stick pan with cooking oil spray; cook meatballs until browned all over.

Combine meatballs, undrained crushed tomatoes, Tomato Supreme and stock in 3-litre (12-cup) ovenproof dish. Bake, covered, in moderate oven 45 minutes. Gently stir in pasta; bake, covered, about 20 minutes or until pasta is tender.

glossary

almond meal also known as ground almonds.

beef

blade steak: from the shoulder blade area.

chuck steak: from the neck.

minced: also known as ground beef.

round steak: otherwise termed the knuckle or thick flank, from the front portion of the thigh or the hind leg.

breadcrumbs

stale: one- or two-day-old bread made into crumbs by grating, blending or processing.

capsicum also known as bell pepper.

cayenne pepper a thin-fleshed, long, extremely hot red chilli; usually purchased dried and ground.

chicken

drumstick: leg with skin intact.

thigh cutlet: thigh with skin and centre bone intact; also known as a chicken chop.

chickpeas also called garbanzos.

couscous a fine, grain-like cereal product, made from semolina.

daikon a basic food in Japan, it is also called giant white radish.

eggplant also known as aubergine.

fish sauce also called nam pla or nuoc nam; made from pulverised salted fermented fish.

flour, plain an all-purpose flour, made from wheat.

garam masala a blend of spices, originating in north India; based on varying proportions of cardamom, cinnamon, cloves, coriander, fennel and cumin, roasted and ground together. Black pepper and chilli can be added for a hotter version.

green ginger wine alcoholic sweet wine infused with finely ground ginger.

hoisin sauce a thick, sweet and spicy Chinese paste made from salted fermented soy beans, onions and garlic.

kumara Polynesian name of orange-fleshed sweet potato.

lamb

chump chop: the cut from just above the hind legs to the mid-loin section; it can be used as a piece for roasting or cut into chops.

cutlet: small, tender rib chop.

French-trimmed lamb shanks: also known as drumsticks or Frenched shanks; all the gristle at narrow end of the bone is discarded and the remaining meat trimmed.

shank: forequarter leg.

okra also known as bhindi, bamia or lady's fingers; a green, ridged, oblong pod with a furry skin. Native to Africa, this vegetable is used in Indian, Middle-eastern and Creole dishes.

onion

green: also known as scallion or (incorrectly) shallot; an immature onion picked before the bulb has formed, having a long, bright-green edible stalk.

red: also known as Spanish or Bermuda onion

spring: has narrow green-leafed top and a fairly large sweet white bulb.

pancetta an Italian salt-cured pork roll, usually cut

from the belly. Bacon can be substituted.

paprika ground dried red capsicum (bell pepper), available sweet or hot.

pasta, risoni small rice-shaped pasta.

polenta a flour-like cereal made of ground corn (maize); similar to cornmeal but coarser and darker in colour; also the name of the dish made from it.

rice

basmati: a white, fragrant long-grained rice. It should be washed several times before cooking.

long-grain: elongated grain, remains separate when cooked; most popular steaming rice in Asia.

sambal oelek (also ulek or olek) Indonesian in origin; a salty paste made from ground chillies, sugar and spices.

seasoned pepper a combination of black pepper, garlic flakes, red capsicum, paprika and garlic.

soy sauce made from fermented soy beans. Several variations are available in most supermarkets and Asian food stores, among them

are salt-reduced, light, sweet and salty.

spinach correct name for spinach; the green vegetable often called spinach is correctly known as Swiss chard, sliverbeet or seakale.

star anise a dried star-shaped pod whose seeds have an astringent aniseed flavour.

stock 1 cup (250ml) stock is the equivalent of 1 cup (250ml) water plus 1 crumbled stock cube (or 1 teaspoon stock powder).

sultanas golden raisins.

tomato

paste: triple-concentrated tomato puree used to flavour soups, stews, sauces and casseroles.

puree: canned pureed tomatoes (not tomato paste). Substitute with fresh peeled and pureed tomatoes.

sauce: also known as ketchup or catsup; a flavoured condiment made from tomatoes, vinegar and spices.

supreme: a canned product

consisting of tomatoes, onions, celery, peppers, cheese and seasonings.

veal meat from a young calf, identified by its creamy pink flesh, fine texture and delicate taste.

cutlet: choice chop from the mid-loin (back) area.

loin chop: from a shortloin rib.

osso bucco: this famous Italian dish uses the hind or forequarter shank or knuckle cut into medallions. When the knuckle is trimmed of meat at the thin end, this is known as a "Frenched" knuckle.

yogurt, low fat, plain we used yogurt with a fat content of less than 0.2%.

zucchini also known as courgette.

facts and figures

These conversions are approximate only, but the difference between an exact and the approximate conversion of various liquid and dry measures is minimal and will not affect your cooking results.

Measuring equipment

The difference between one country's measuring cups and another's is, at most, within a 2 or 3 teaspoon variance. (For the record, 1 Australian metric measuring cup holds approximately 250ml.) The most accurate way of measuring dry ingredients is to weigh them. For liquids, use a clear glass or plastic jug having metric markings.

Note: NZ, Canada, USA and UK all use 15ml tablespoons. Australian tablespoons measure 20ml.
All cup and spoon measurements are level.

How to measure

When using graduated measuring cups, shake dry ingredients loosely into the appropriate cup. Do not tap the cup on a bench or tightly pack the ingredients unless directed to do so. Level the top of measuring cups and measuring spoons with a knife. When measuring liquids, place a clear glass or plastic jug having metric markings on a flat surface to check accuracy at eye level.

Dry Measures

metric	imperial
15g	1/2oz
30g	1oz
60g	2oz
90g	3oz
125g	4oz (1/4lb)
155g	5oz
185g	6oz
220g	7oz
250g	8oz (1/2lb)
280g	9oz
315g	10oz
345g	11oz
375g	12oz (3/4lb)
410g	13oz
440g	14oz
470g	15oz
500g	16oz (1lb)
750g	24oz (11/2lb)
1kg	32oz (2lb)

We use large eggs having an average weight of 60g.

Liquid Measures

metric	imperial
30ml	1 fluid oz
60ml	2 fluid oz
100ml	3 fluid oz
125ml	4 fluid oz
150ml	5 fluid oz (1/4 pint/1 gill)
190ml	6 fluid oz
250ml (1cup)	8 fluid oz
300ml	10 fluid oz (1/2 pint)
500ml	16 fluid oz
600ml	20 fluid oz (1 pint)
1000ml (1litre)	13/4 pints

Helpful Measures

metric	imperial
3mm	1/8in
6mm	1/4in
1cm	1/2in
2cm	3/4in
2.5cm	1in
6cm	21/2in
8cm	3in
20cm	8in
23cm	9in
25cm	10in
30cm	12in (1ft)

Oven Temperatures

These oven temperatures are only a guide.
Always check the manufacturer's manual.

	C°(Celsius)	F°(Fahrenheit)	Gas Mark
Very slow	120	250	1
Slow	150	300	2
Moderately slow	160	325	3
Moderate	180 –190	350 – 375	4
Moderately hot	200 – 210	400 – 425	5
Hot	220 – 230	450 – 475	6
Very hot	240 – 250	500 – 525	7

Food editor Pamela Clark
Associate food editor Karen Hammial
Assistant food editor Kathy McGarry
Assistant recipe editor Elizabeth Hooper
Home Library Staff
Editor-in-chief Mary Coleman
Marketing manager Nicole Pizanis
Editor Susan Tomnay
Subeditor Bianca Martin
Concept design Jackie Richards
Designer Sue de Guingand
Group publisher Paul Dykzeul

Produced by *The Australian Women's Weekly* Home Library, Sydney.
Colour separations by ACP Colour Graphics Pty Ltd, Sydney.
Printing by Diamond Press Limited, Sydney.
Published by ACP Publishing Pty Limited, 54 Park St, Sydney;
GPO Box 4088, Sydney, NSW 1028. Ph: (02) 9282 8618 Fax: (02) 9267 9438.
AWWHomeLib@publishing.acp.com.au
Australia: Distributed by Network Distribution Company,
GPO Box 4088, Sydney, NSW 1028. Ph: (02) 9282 8777 Fax: (02) 9264 3278.
United Kingdom: Distributed by Australian Consolidated Press (UK),
Moulton Park Business Centre, Red House Rd, Moulton Park, Northampton, NN3 6AQ.
Ph: (01604) 497 531 Fax: (01604) 497 533 Acpukltd@aol.com
Canada: Distributed by Whitecap Books Ltd,
351 Lynn Ave, North Vancouver, BC, V7J 2C4, (604) 980 9852.
New Zealand: Distributed by Netlink Distribution Company,
17B Hargreaves St, Level 5, College Hill, Auckland 1, (9) 302 7616.
South Africa: Distributed by PSD Promotions (Pty) Ltd,
PO Box 1175, Isando 1600, SA, (011) 392 6065.

Healthy Eating: Casseroles

Includes index.
ISBN 1 86396 125 9.

1Casserole cookery. I Title: Australian Women's Weekly.
(Series: Australian Women's Weekly healthy eating mini series).
641.821

ACP Publishing Pty Limited 1999
ACN 053 273 546

This publication is copyright. No part of it may be reproduced or transmitted
in any form without the written permission of the publishers.

Cover: Tagine of beef with tomatoes, page 31.
Photographer Scott Cameron
Back cover: Boeuf bourguignon, page 23.